UNDER THE BLUE SKY

LYRICS FROM MY SONGS

LAURIAN TALER

GONG PUBLISHING
TORONTO

BY THE SAME AUTHOR

ALMOST ESSENTIALS
ON A BLADE OF GRASS
SO MANY WORDS
SAGACITY

UNDER THE BLUE SKY
LYRICS FROM MY SONGS

©Laurian Taler, 2014

GONG PUBLISHING
TORONTO

www.gongnog.com

ISBN 978-1-926477-03-9

Laurian Taler

Under the blue skies,
Depending where you are,
Clouds cover or they bar
The view of your eyes.
That's why sometimes
One can't see
Infinity.

Under the Blue Sky

PREFACE

There are so many things happening under the blue sky. Actually, everything that happens to us goes on under there. I chose this title for my last volume of lyrics from my songs because of a song named "Living under the smoky sky", whose lyrics I left out of the collection. However, it made me write a few lines of poetry which were placed on page 3 in lieu of dedication. Of course, those lines are the dedication. You may relate to the fact that clouds appear in everyone's life and those clouds impede the view that most of us cherish. Whatever happens under the blue sky becomes, directly or not, part of our lives. And since my songs have tried to capture, both in music and in words, snippets of life's happenings, I thought that the title might cover them all. Of course, there are different shades of grey in the clouds, as there are different amounts of trouble in anyone's life. That's why some lyrics capture this with song names that suggest such states of spirit. The readers might find recognition of their own states of spirit or feelings at one time or another, especially when falling into what we call with two consonants and two vowels, of which one is silent, love.

No matter whether the reader is only eleven years old or is approaching the century, the lyrics, taken together with the songs available elsewhere, (on www.gongnog.com) will undoubtedly provoke some profound vibrations and will allow for a better understanding of life's delicate journeys.

Under the Blue Sky

TABLE OF CONTENTS

NR. CD/Position Song   Page

2202. BE MINE FOREVER

Music & lyrics ©Laurian Taler, 2006

A1
Be mine forever, only mine,
In candlelight you always shine,
At dusk or when the sun is bright
You bring me that romantic night

A2
Be mine forever, only mine,
When I'm awake, when with you dine
Your smile brings rapture to my soul
Your presence makes my life so whole

B
When I'm with you, oh, how can it be
Feeling the bliss in eternity
I do not want it to go away
All that deep charm that you do convey
Just holding hands tight, even by chance
Gives in my heart such a resonance

I know it's you who I want to bless
As you bring me all this huge happiness

A1, A2

2203. WHEN MY BABY JUST SMILES

Music & lyrics ©Laurian Taler, 2006
A
When my baby just smiles to me
When my baby caresses me
All the sudden I feel so hot
And I get red in cheeks a lot

When my baby laughs beautiful
When my baby says I am cool
I get tingling under my chin
And I'm ready to think of sin

B
Whatever happens
I am no more in control
Of myself
I want to conquer for my baby
All the big world
And herself
I want to fly her to stars
I want to make her a queen
I want to feel with her all,
Yang and Yin

A
When my baby just smiles to me
When my baby caresses me
All the sudden I feel so hot
And I get red in cheeks a lot

When my baby laughs beautiful
When my baby says I am cool
I get tingling under my chin
And I'm ready to think of sin

2204. GROWING OLD AND GREEN

Music & lyrics ©Laurian Taler, 2005

A1
Growing old and green
Shouldn't be so hard
Life should be still
A right mix of fun

A2
Growing old and green
Shouldn't be so hard
Wrinkles and some pain
Bear them all

B1
Surrounded by all your family
Drinking with gusto the prescribed tea
Eating what is fresh, moderately
Learning not to complain

B2
Keeping everything simple and plain
Conscious-wise being without a stain
Exercising limbs and also mind
And acting kind

A1, A2

2205. COME BACK TO ME

A1
Come back to me
Come back to me
Without you I can't live
Come back to me
Come back to me
To you my love I'll give

B
With your deep eyes you have conquered me
And then laughing you have left
Without words
You've encountered your share of
Bad luck
Now you need serenity

C (2x)
I need you so, my love
I need you so, my love
I need you so, my love
Need you so, need you so, need you so

A1, B

2206. I DREAMED OF YOU AGAIN

Music & lyrics ©Laurian Taler, 2006

A
I dreamed of you again
It felt so good
You were so young again
And in the mood
You smiled a lot to me
And so caressed
That I knew ecstasy
Climbed to a higher crest

B
Dreaming, dreaming that I have
From you the love that you gave me
Makes me enchanted as I was
When you believed my babe to be

A, B

2207. MORNINGS ARE JUST FOR LOVERS

Music & lyrics ©Laurian Taler, 2006

A
Mornings are just for lovers
They awake in a daze
Mornings are just for lovers
Their love deep in haze
Lovers wake up and shiver
Asking if they have fever
Trembling still for each other
After a night of bliss

B
One will cook scrambled eggs
Barely up on their legs
Knowing you must replenish
Before it can vanish
The blind frazzle-dazzle,
The other 's strength,
You beware, love
It's daybreak

A, B

2208. I WANTED YOU

Music & lyrics ©Laurian Taler, 2006

A1
I wanted you because I loved you
I wanted you to be my love
I wanted you because my heart said
You are the one that will fill my life with happiness
A2
I wanted you because I loved you
I wanted you to be my love
I wanted you because my heart said
You are the one that I will love

B
Time has passed and you
Have given me a no, no sign
I was left in limbo and you're still, still, not mine
Life's short, what's going, what's gonna be then
Going our separate ways
Life's short, what's going, what's gonna be then
In your life and in my life

A3
I still want you because I love you
I still want you to be my love
I still want you because my heart says
You are the one that will fill my life with happiness

2209. WE HAVE MET IN PARADISE

Music & lyrics ©Laurian Taler, 2006

A
We have met in Paradise
You were beautiful and wise
I was wild in love with you
And the skies were always blue

B
When we looked for other fields
We discovered we need shields
To protect our outer crust
To avoid biting the dust
A small heaven we then built
Where happiness we spilled, yeah,
A small heaven we then built
Where happiness we spilled

A, B

2210. IT'S ANOTHER SONG

Music & lyrics ©Laurian Taler, 2005

A (2x)
It's another song
Like many among
Those that sing again
Sadness and pain
For break in love

'Cause a break in love
Is a break of heart
And you know how hurt
Are you just when
Suffering it.

B
What do you do
When passion dies
Though you don't want,
Slowly in pain

Can you find some
Form of relief
For a rebirth

What do you do
When passion dies
Slowly in pain

Can you find some
Form of relief
For a rebirth

A

2301. SUMMER

A1
Summer
Where are you hot summer
I want you, hot summer,
With beaches and rain
With walks in twilight
With sky by stars light
With you beside me
Two bodies enchain

A2
Summer
Come faster, oh, summer
I need you, oh, summer
To bring me sun's heat
Go down to seashore
Frolic like before
With you beside me
And love to complete

B
With you beside me
It's summer again
With you beside seasons
Pass like a train
With you beside me
I feel that you guide me
Of bad things you hide me
And keep me so sane

A1, A2

2302. RETURN TO ME NOW YOU CAN

Music & lyrics ©Laurian Taler, 2006, 2008

A1
Return to me, now you can,
After a life
Has flown away between us
A life with so much fracas
Return to me, now you can

A2
Return to me, it's not late,
To feel my heart
That waited for you so long
That knew for whom you belong
Return to me, I still wait

B1
I can understand that you are
So down on your luck
And you feel so struck
Trying to avert
Yet another hurt
Return to me, now you can

B2
(instrumental)

A1
Return to me, now you can,
Become my love
You can renew our bond
To my love you can respond
Return to me, now you can

2303. YOUR EYES ONLY

Music & lyrics ©Laurian Taler, 2008

A1
Your eyes only can see what
I'm writing for you
Your eyes only can see what
Is tormenting me

A2
Your eyes only can see what
Fight goes through my soul
Your eyes only can
Your eyes only can see what
Is my tender goal

B (2x)
Read, see how deep are
Those strong feelings just for you
I keep them so well hidden
From all eyes
Maybe you'll find how
To answer back to my love
It's only what I hope for
From your eyes

2304. WHAT ELSE YOU'LL DO FOR ME

Music & lyrics ©Laurian Taler, 2011

What else you'll do (4x)

A1
What else you'll do for me
Apart from saying -Gee,
I'll bring you gold and silver
And the moon off the sky

A2
What else you'll do for me
Better act tenderly
My soul aches for caresses
And for the truth of love

B
I can't wait
(2x)
Don't try to deceive
Make me to believe
That your love's as true
As my love

A1, A2, B

C
(2x)
Hold my hands
And look straight into my eyes
Without a blink
Then hold me tightly

C (So) A1, A2, B

2305. MY LOVE FOR YOU

Music & lyrics ©Laurian Taler, 2007

A1
My love for you / Doesn't have bounds
My love for you / Flies over mounds
My love for you / Trembles in night
My love for you /Grows at your sight
My love for you /Keeps my heart right

A2
Your love for me / Is elixir
Your love for me / Is so sincere
Your love for me / My songs inspire
Your love for me / Gives me the fire
Your love for me / Gives me the fire
To love you (4x)

B1
In the wilderness of life
You are my only refuge
Friend and lover, and then wife
With me till the last deluge
With me till the last deluge
Beautifying wherever you walk
Make me get over any roadblock
You inspire/ My desire / And you fill
My dream empire
With all your love (3x)

A2

2306. THINK A BIT, GET REAL

Music & lyrics ©Laurian Taler, 2008, 2011

A1
Think a bit, get real
You must not conceal
What your feelings truly are
It's time to resemble
Like the leafs in wind
That tremble
When emotions spar

A2
Think a bit, life passes
You don't get the classes
To teach you that love's a mess
On your feet you try it
In your head you sigh it
'Cause it will make you obsess

B1
But without love what's life
Just a pile of raw strife
And an endless stinking chore
Think a bit, get real
Grow out of ordeal
So that you can shout Amor

B2
Fall in love, be dashing
You can look so smashing
Carry yourself glamourous
Think a bit, get real
You can sure deal
A relation amorous

2307. WHO IS AT THE DOOR

Music & lyrics ©Laurian Taler, 2007

A1
Guess, who's at the door
Check, it's what you hope
Or another sore
Who's trying to sell you dope

A2
Guess, who's at the door
Will you suffer more
Or you'll learn to cope
If you want to have some hope

B1
Your door is your valuable shield
It puts a wall toward the unknown
Behind it with power you wield
It gives you a safety zone

B2
Beware, there are so many doors,
Some you keep open without force
Some you keep shut to remain whole
And maintain sane your deep soul

Da capo

2308. MELODY'S RETURN

Music & lyrics ©Laurian Taler, 2007, 2011

A1
I hope, I pray
All night and day
For Melody's return
It's not a girl
But it's a swirl
And my one main concern

'Cause I can't stand
Whatever band
That makes from songs a noise
Instead of singing melodies
To enchant and bring joys

A2
The queen of music
Is not rhythm
It is song's purity
That brings out
Feelings hidden long
In soul with harmony
That's why I hope
I even pray
For Melody's return
Else what we'd have
Would be soul's death
And ashes in an urn

B (2x)
Life is nothing without melody
It's the songs that bring us joy
Up lifting all that we so much feel
And put in life much more zeal

2309. UNDER THE TREES

Music & lyrics ©Laurian Taler, 2007, 2010

A1
Under the trees where we kissed
And so discovered lovers exist
We said sweet words that we believed
Not knowing yet how long they lived

A2
Under the trees we made a pact
That we'll keep love for us intact
That we'll walk hand in hand till end
Together life with love we'll spend

B
We didn't know that to keep love alive
We must be strong and together must strive
Not just say words but make sure our deeds
Show that love's attraction must be mixed
With utmost care and high respect

A3
The trees have changed their green leaves
And we have changed under our sleeves
We cared less, we showed neglect
We lost the most of high respect

A4
The trees have changed their green leaves
We stole our chances just like low thieves
As we forgot what we have said
Sweet words that died now love is dead

2310. THERE IS NO FAITH

Music & lyrics ©Laurian Taler, 2009

A1
There is no faith, there is no faith
In humanity
There is no faith, there is no faith
In reality
There is just faith, there is wrong faith
In divinity
There is wrong faith, there is wrong faith
In infinity

B
Brainwashed from childhood
To believe in what is not
Robbed by traditions
From a past that erred a lot
Some people pray gods
Some people kill for
A life forever in an after life
Losing their reason
They commit treason
And strife

A2, B2, A3

Laurian Taler

2401. COME HAPPY DAYS

Music & lyrics ©Laurian Taler, 2011, 2014

A
What sunny days you bring
When you smile and you sing
But how dark are the nights
When we fall into fights

(2x)
Oh I so wish that only sunny
Stay our days for us
And our nights are
Only for the swing

B
Come happy days much faster
Bring warmth as you can master
Oh I so wish that only sunny
Stay our days for us
And our nights are
Only for the swing
Oh I so wish that only sunny
Stay our days for us
And our nights are
Only for the swing, the swing

2402. ANOTHER DREAM

Music & lyrics ©Laurian Taler, 2008

A1
Another dream, another sky,
Another creed, another why,
Another cloud around my goal
Another storm inside my soul
A2
Another daze, another craze,
Another base, another maze,
How will I get out from this maze
And overcome this crazy phase

B
Will I return soon to reality
Will I see, will I see facts clearly
Dreams are the dark side
I must now decide
Get rid of strife
And get back to my life

A3
Another dream, I want to scream,
My mind asleep creates a creep,
I must wake up, I must work up,
I must build up my own esteem

A4
Give me your hand, give me a rope,
With your strong arm I may just cope
I'll clean my act, I don't need dope
Just give me hope, give me some hope

2403. LOST SAIL

Music & lyrics ©Laurian Taler, 2014

A1
Rowing on some turbulent waves
We may rich islands with graves and raves
Rowing when smooth and when in a gale
We feel like we have lost sail

A2
Life's a dance on the up and the down
Carry your jacket as not to drown
Make sure you have with what to out bail
Even if you lost your sail

B (2x)
Hold tight, the waves will calm,
Hold tight, life's in your palms,
Hold tight at any cost
With hope you are never lost

A1, A2, B (2x)

2404. WE SOMETIMES CRY

Music & lyrics ©Laurian Taler, 2014

A1
We sometimes cry
During our dreams
When seem to fly
Releasing screams
We try to cling
To some fake wings
Of unspoken desire

A2
It is those wings
Feathered with hope
To which we cling
As if a rope
That saves the night
From our flight
To reach for so much higher

B (2X)
Shy away from dreams
Full of fire
Shy away from dreams
Of desire

A1, A2

2405. BERLIN

Music & lyrics ©Laurian Taler, 2009

A
Berlin,
Going through blocks of stone
And looking down the shelves
Of burned books emptiness
You made me cry again
You made me hope again
For mankind
Berlin, Berlin

B
With your large streets and tall houses
You let thoughts light flow
If you make anew your culture
All mankind to glow
With your renewed adoration
For embracing good
You may give the world elation
To best improve its mood
    best improve its mood
      best improve its mood

A2
Berlin,
From marsh to marching bands
From arches to green lands
And full of rich marble
You pass from past to now
You step with your know how
In new times
Berlin, Berlin

2406. BUILD ME A MAP

Music & lyrics ©Laurian Taler, 2009

A1
Build me a map
Of the world
Without the wars
Build me a map
Of the world
Healthy, of course

B1 (2X)
Build me a map to shine
All children 's eyes divine
To show they grow in peace
With love around

B2
Build me a map to see
All people being free
Working for their needs
Without wrong creeds

C (2X)
You cannot rest on a planet
Where is so much to do
Keep acting goodness to happen
Goodness and freedom that's true

A1, B1 (2x)

Do your part and be happy
Do your part and be happy
Do your part and be happy
Now

2407. EARLY CALL

Music & lyrics ©Laurian Taler, 2009, 2014

A1
I heard when young an early call
I had to sit and write to my doll
She never, never answered back
'Cause I had asked her to my sack

A2
Show that what you have
Can withstand the challenge
The early call that through me ran
Was sign I turned to be a man
But look, it's not enough to write
To get your love down for a night

B
A man understands that love is
For a life, not just a night
That is how you build what bliss is
When with patience
Bring forward your life plight
Show that what you feel
Can keep up the balance
Show that what you know
Can hold high your loved one
For eternity

A2, B

2408. MILK AND HONEY

Music & lyrics ©Laurian Taler, 2011

A1
A land where flow
The honey and milk
And where the sky
Is free and blue silk
The stars have six tips
Smiles are on folks' lips
With beauty' n their eyes
And people so wise

A2
In this land was born
The story of mankind
Where people learned
For justice and mind
To conquer the unknown
Create harmony
Sharing what they own
For life's quality

B
Oy, there were times when all life was hard
Folks were exiled, became slaves
But they have developed strong survival skills
We are their heirs and now here stand guard

A3
Shalom Israel
Hope for aged and young
Shalom Israel
From old to new tongue

Shalom Israel (3x)
You' ll always prevail

A4
Shalom Israel
Your greeting means Peace
With wisdom you work
To shine and increase
Shalom Israel (3x)
You' ll always prevail.

2409. GIVE IT A GOOD TRY

Music & lyrics ©Laurian Taler, 2010

A1
Give it a good try, play fair, it won't hurt,
Make it your own try, play fair, 'cause you need
To grow with your tries, fair play and mistakes
'Cause without them, you won't be you
You'll become you when trying hard

A2
Plan what you do, 'cause life is awful short
Use all the time to reach to your planned port
Do it with all the passion that you store
And ask for more, and ask for more
Just from yourself you ask for more

B
Life's only the play you write
Life's only the game in sight
And life plays games with you
And the game has hard rules too
Play the game by the rules of fair play

A1, A2

2410. WE WERE BOUND
(You told me many lies)

Music & lyrics ©Laurian Taler, 2009

A1
You told me many lies
'Cause you were full of vice
I listened and I thought
That you were ever hot

A2
It mattered not to me
That beyond lies I'd see
A troubled soul that tried
Behind these lies to hide

B1
What it really mattered was that
You could change my life
What it really mattered was that
I could change your life
What it really mattered was that
We were bound for life
We were bound for life
And for true love

2501. ZAZIE RUMBA

Music & lyrics ©Laurian Taler, 2007, 2010

A1
Zazie's a girl that arrived from afar
Zazie works nights in a men - only bar
And she works days what she can with no qualms
She sends money back home to her mom

A2
Zazie will dance with whomever will pay
Daily or nightly for dough she will lay
Zazie will do just whatever you want
Vainly hoping she won't be a taunt

B1
She does this to help all her siblings
Of which she has got more than eight
'Cause with the two of her own little children
She must provide for a dozen poor souls

B2
Zazie could well be like you or me
But life threw her in such turmoil
Don't judge her wrong, or look her
Down, contemptuous
Stretch your hand, welcome her on our soil

A1

2502. YOU SMILED

Music & lyrics ©Laurian Taler, 2007

A1
You smiled and made light
You smiled and a flame
Turned on in my heart
And I can't set it apart

A2
You laughed and I saw
A string of white pearls
Enchanting your face
And taking me out of place

B
You catapulted me into the sky
I'm a heavenly body
I am a planet that swirls around you
As you are my bright star

A1, A2, B

2503. I FORGOT FLOWERS

Music & lyrics ©Laurian Taler, 2010

A
I forgot flowers
Have such meaning powers
When given or not given too
For what is simple and true
Hope and intense expectation
For durable, faithful love
Faithful love
Give from the heart
As you show your affection
And how enchanted you ' are
'Cause flowers have this fragrance and colours
To wildly turn many heads
Just don't forget that with a flower
You should not hurt

B
Flowers can
Bring the delicate feelings from you
Can refresh a relation you lost
Or that you wish
Oh, so dearly to reconnect
For passion and all

2504. YOU SAVE ME FROM MYSELF

Music & lyrics ©Laurian Taler, 2007, 2010

A1
You save me from myself
Just with your smile
And your deep sigh,
A tremor in my heart
Is what you do
With your eyes' light

B1
 You amaze me with
Your strange way of walking
You put me in trance
With your soft way of talking
You create vibrations
That I did not know
Make me tremor with
A golden glow

A2
You save me from myself
As I am so
Lost in the wood
You are the only one
Who have seen deep
And understood

B2
You have pulled me up
From the marsh of doubting
You took me along
The hard climb of the mountain
And you showed me how

Under the Blue Sky

I must look at the sky
Even only with
My own mind's eye
Even only with
My own mind's eye
Even only with
My own mind's eye

2505. ON MY FIELD

Music & lyrics ©Laurian Taler, 2010

A1
On my field surrounded by willow trees
I imagined building our nest
Where in a hammock under the willow trees
I saw your sweet, darling smile

B1
So, I gathered all my power
And I started putting roots down
I turned grains in sacs of flour
To buy with your dressing gown

A2
On my field surrounded by willow trees
We spread with friends our joyfulness
It was there we worked like the bees
To grow old in happiness

B2
It took us two generations
To change that field into a town
As our kids with high aspirations
Made it a place of renown

2506. BURDEN

Music & lyrics ©Laurian Taler, 2010, 2014

A
Burden I hold
A fretting heart
That beats now weak
And now much too bold
Thinking that you,
Who loved my art,
Decided to seek
Love à la carte

B
My burden feels
From head to heels
Heavy at night
When you come in sight
A ghost that I try hard to get rid
A burden that I try to forbid

A2
There you are
My mind paints you
An image that
Keeps coming through
It weighs me down
Ready to drown
Whatever feelings
I want to frown.

B

2507. YOU GAVE ME JUST WHAT I NEEDED

Music & lyrics ©Laurian Taler, 2010

A1
You gave me just what I needed
With a glance that said so much
You gave me just what I needed
With a touch beyond a touch

You gave me so much (2x)

A2
You gave me just what I needed
A desire to fight all
You gave me just what I needed
The belief I'll reach my goal

You gave me so much (2x)

B1
As you trusted, with intuition
Whatever my foolish plans were
I became sure that no matter what is
You will always understand

B2
And you showed me much greater patience
Whenever I made those mistakes
Which could have ruined all those strong bonds that
Kept us together so long

You gave me all

2508. WILL YOU CHOOSE ME FOR YOUR LOVE

Music & lyrics ©Laurian Taler, 2010

A1
Will you choose me for your love
If love blossomed in your soul
If your glance falls on my face
And my song may start your heart race

A2
Will you choose me for your love
In a world that needs much love
In a world where we can build
For all lovers a strong shield (3x)

B1
Your heart and my heart will beat in a frenzy
With the songs that we will sing
Your mind and my mind will write
Our story that will embellish mankind
It will be a model of beauty
It will be a model of love
It will be a model of meaning
The meaning that is coming only from love

A1, A2

2509. A SONG FOR THE SINGLE CROWD

Music & lyrics ©Laurian Taler, 2007, 2011

A1
A song for the single crowd
For those that have never vowed
To love and be loved
To tie tight their hearts
To see in their mates
The world

A2
A song for the single soul
The one that keeps in control
Of freedom of same
To play so well the game
To be on the roll
With love

B1
Say you do not want to hear
Lectures on commitments -
Well,
Don't expect the world to love you, dear,
Just 'cause you want
Without giving what you have best
Lonely heart
Without giving what you have best
Lonely heart

2510. OLD FRIENDS ARE BETTER

Music & lyrics ©Laurian Taler, 2010

dedicated to Beru, at 70 years of true friendship

A1
Old friends are better than the new ones
Old friends are sure to be close
Old friends are always what you hope for
Old friends are loyal to the end

A2
Old friends will listen to your laments
Old friends will shake you out of mud
You are such friend, that's why I love you
More like a brother than a friend

B
Old friends, you can heal a deep wound with them
Old friends, you can tell bad jokes without hurt
Old friends will understand your hunger now
For the ties that bind the soul (3x)

1801. DAYDREAMS

Music & lyrics ©Laurian Taler, 2011

A1
Daydreams surround my head
My eyes just stare
Looking as far as they can see no more

Daydreams mesmerize me
With wishful thinking
Taking me in a realm where I still hope

Only it's still a fuzzy hope in vain (2x)

A2
Daydreams move with the speed
Of snails on moon light
Parallel universe that flips my mind

Daydreams turn upside down
The rules of reason
Giving me what I breathe from dawn to dusk

And then I turn to real nightly dreams (2x)

1804. GIULIA

Music & lyrics ©Laurian Taler, 2001, 2011

A
Giulia
Child from a dream
Giulia
Child from a dream
I don't know how to revert
All the days and nights I dreamt you
I don't know how to erase
All the visions of your face

B
Songs and poems with your name
Have been written over long time
Maybe those were not for you
Although many knew your splendour
My words I know come from heart
Even if they can't describe you
As your beauty goes beyond
What a song can praise all your charm

LEAVE THE EARTH

Music & lyrics ©Laurian Taler, 2007
(from the musical "ONE EARTH")

For now we hold only one choice
To have a better planet
For now we hold only one choice
To care for our planet

Leave the Earth
Or live on Earth
I made up my mind
Leave the Earth
Or live on Earth
Earth's one of a kind

Leave the Earth
Or live on Earth
You do what you need
Leave the Earth
Or live on Earth
And care it indeed

ONE EARTH

Music & lyrics ©Laurian Taler, 2007
(from the musical "ONE EARTH")

A1
One Earth
Is all we have
For us and for who'll come
One Earth
Is all we have
For us and for who'll come

A2
A garden for
Our mankind
To care with love
A sacred place
We must dwell
We must hold so dear
To our hearts

B1
Une terre
C'est tout qu'avons
Pour nous et ceux qui viennent
Une terre
C'est tout qu'avons
Pour nous et ceux qui viennent

B2
Jardin pour tous,
Pour tout le monde
Que nous soignons
Endroit sacré

Pour tenir
Tellement chère
La terre
À nos vrais coeurs

C
If we don't act now
We won't have our air
We won't have our water
We won't have our earth

We must save our land
We must save our water
We must save our air
We must save ourselves

2603. GOING FROM HERE TO NOWHERE

Music & lyrics ©Laurian Taler, 2011, 2013

A1
Going from here to nowhere
As fast and as far I can
Tearing down what I most care
In a life that I can't plan

I realize that I'm crazy
No kind of help I accept
That my mind is always hazy
As if for years I slept

B1
Wake me, wake me
Shake me, shake me
Hold me, hold me
In your strong arms,

Help me, help me
Give me power
To return now
To your sane charms

I so love, YAY!

A2
Going from nowhere to here
As fast and as well I can
Building up what I most care
Is what a life I must plan
I realize I was crazy

Laurian Taler

Your steadfast help to reject
Now my mind is no more lazy
Your love in it I detect

B2
Wake me, wake me
Shake me, shake me
Hold me, hold me
In your strong arms,

Help me, help me
Give me power
I return now
To your sane charms

I so love, YAY!

2604. JOY CAME FROM A WALTZ

Music & lyrics ©Laurian Taler, 2011

A1
Joy came from a waltz
That we slow danced together
Yes, joy came from holding
Your body 'n my arms
Joy came from the beat
That our hearts beat together
While my eyes were singing
When watching your charms

B1
Nobody gave me that joy
Nobody will give such joy
Nobody gave me that joy
While dancing a waltz

A2
Joy comes from some little
Events that surround us
Yes, joy comes from smiling
At strangers and friends
Joy comes when we do what
Life asks us to accomplish
To make others happy
No matter how ends

B2
Everybody should enjoy
Life without some dirty ploy
Everybody should enjoy
What love brings to us

2606. A PINK DREAM

Music & lyrics ©Laurian Taler, 2011, 2013

A1
I had a rosy dream
A pink dream last night
I had a rosy dream
I can't describe- Yeah
It was a rosy dream
Because I only
Remember it was you
Who wore some pink
You only wore a lipstick
On your lips

You only wore a lipstick on
Your rosy lips

A2
I had a rosy dream
A pink dream last night
You were surrounded by
Pink, rosy guys (girls)- Yeah
Why were they around you
It's beyond question
How comfortable could
I be of that?
You seemed to be so proud
Of all around

I think I went in the pink dream
Out of my mind

A3
Don't give me rosy dreams
Or pink dreams no more
Better be like I always dream
Of you- Yeah

Be only you, just you, just you
In my dreams
Whatever colour be, except of pink
A dream is just a dream,
It's true, I think
But I can't stand no dreams
That come sudden in pink.

2607. ASK ME WHAT I REALLY KNOW

A
Ask me what I really know
About the path on which I go
And If it is good
The fact I take it through the woods,
At night,
If I can withstand a fight
In many dangers I must confront
From the hindrances that in life
I must find a way to survive

B
I don't have
Answers to these
Simple questions that you may ask
What I know is that I will
Try to hold firm on to what I want
And make sure none gets hurt
And keep clean my face out of dirt
Learn how things connect, how they whirled
And build for my brethren
A good world.

A, B

2608. SLOW JOY

Music & lyrics ©Laurian Taler, 2011

A
Between a hard place and anvil
Life runs its due course with such speed
That you seem to gasp for fresh air
Trying from it all to be freed

(2x)
That's when a slow joy
With its multiple embraces
Warmly surrounds you
With a feel that feels so true

B
Take your time to learn the enjoyment
Of the slower pace you can live
You will see that life is more precious
And you even more can achieve

(2x)
That's when a slow joy
With its multiple embraces
Warmly surrounds you
With a feel that feels so true

2609. ASK AGAIN

Music & lyrics ©Laurian Taler, 2013

A1
Ask again / The word that yet
I can't pronounce
Ask again / For that feeling
I can't advance
It will come a time / That I will say
The words you want
And then you will
Know for sure
That I mean each word

A2
Do not ask
To lie so you
Can be assured
Do not ask
To tell you what
It's not my task
Be afraid of those
Who trick you
With sweet words that lie
Be afraid of
Those who promise
The pie in the sky

B (2x)
Look me straight in face, love,
And in the eyes
I won't say the word, love,
If it's all lies

A1, B (2x)

2610. DO NOT RUSH LOVE

Music & lyrics ©Laurian Taler, 2013

A1
Do not rush love
Don't spoil it
It is a dove
Of smoke
Do not rush love
To-extinguish
The fire that
You stoke

A2
Gingerly touch
Its borders
'Cause it's a smoke
Of dove
Handle not much
In order
Not to disturb
What's love.

B
Love is illusion
A trick that your mind plays
To work up your heart
And waste you away
Love is a potion
That fills with emotion,
Creates a commotion,
Dismay.

A1, A2,
B (2x)

2701. BRING A SHARE

Music & lyrics ©Laurian Taler, 2011, 2013

A1
We've seen around so much evil
That we don't know how to cope
Maybe we need an upheaval
To get from life much more hope
But an upheaval of care
And one of kindness around
So that all life should be fair
And goods for all abound

B1
Bring a share
Of your care
To the world that is your home
Bring a share
Of your care
Keep the peace and say Shalom

A2
You might think peace is not easy
With so much fight everywhere
And that with your work are busy
Time for peace you cannot share
But think of life that can perish
And so much good is destroyed
Sure, if your own life cherish
Fight for all wars to-avoid

2702. ALADDIN

Music & lyrics ©Laurian Taler, 2011, 2013

A
You may have heard of the story of Aladdin
Who found a magic lamp
That if rubbed would release a genie
Who 'd give you want you want
It was for getting his freedom out of bottle
That the genie much aimed
Freedom that we also so much cherish
For which we do magic things

B
As you know, it is just a story
Of the wishful kind
Magic only does develop
In the thinkers' mind
Magic only does develop
In the thinkers' mind

C
The moral of the wonderful Aladdin story
Is that magic may come
In everyone's life when do they fight for
What is just and good
You may dream daily
With most tricky wishful thinking
For magic to arrive
You'll make it come
Through the power of science if
With science strive (4x)

A, B

2703. OH, JAMAICA, REGGAE

A1
Oh, Jamaica, reggae
Is your music right
Oh, Jamaica, reggae
Is your music bright

A2
Oh, Jamaica, reggae
Is your children's song
Oh, Jamaica, reggae
Fighting against wrong

B1
Whenever your children hear reggae
Their hearts beat all for just one hope
Whenever your children hear reggae
It means fight for higher scope

2704. WINTER HEART

Music & lyrics ©Laurian Taler, 2014

A1
Oh, you have a winter heart
For it with a spare part
With which you can torture me
Showing all your cruelty
To enjoy my suffering
And to play me on a string
To turn me into a garbage doll
You can throw when you want to a wall.

A2
Oh, you have an icy heart
With which you tear me apart
You have ice in all your veins
And no feeling in them reigns
My love did not have a chance
To instil in you romance
Between us grew a profound abyss
Winter heart I hope I'll never miss

B
Oh, how cold / Everyone feels
Around you now I know why
Oh, how cold / Everyone feels
Around you now I know why
It's the winter heart in your chest
It's the feelings that you suppressed
Is the icy cold blood
In your heart with a thud
It is the winter heart

A1

2705. BLUE DREAMS

Music & lyrics ©Laurian Taler, 2014

A
I had blue dreams
The same dreams many nights
You were in them a light,
A blue light in my sight
For many nights
A blue angel you were
For many nights in blue
My sleep you did so stir

B
Your light was oh, so easy
Easily spreading on my face
I felt warmed up and dizzy
From your oh, so bluish embrace
Blue were too the smile and the laughter
That came oh, out on your face
Blue were too the arms and the fingers
That tried to touch with grace
In these nights of extremes
My forehead full of blue dreams (3x)

A, B

2706. I LOST ALL SLEEP

Music & lyrics ©Laurian Taler, 2011, 2013

A
I lost all sleep
Since you smiled when I met you
I lost all sleep
Since I told you I like you
What if you
You are smiling like this
Always to those
Who just cross your path

B
What should I do to regain
The lost sleep that you stole from me
How can I find from you without fail
Those feelings for me are true
And even if you now
Tell me the truth
I want to know for how long
You'll bring me peace
And love for a good night sleep

A, B

2707. CRY FOR MOON

Music & lyrics ©Laurian Taler, 2013

A1 (2x)
Cry for moon
With a spoon
Of tears
 Born from love

B
Because love
Rips your heart
It takes
You apart
It will burn
A hole
In what
Is your thought
It will hurt
A lot
To despair
You'll be brought

A2 (2x)
Cry for sun
Till you're done
With tears
 Born from love

B
A3 (2x)
Cry to sky / And then sigh
With tears / Born from love

B

2708. WHAT IS THE MEANING

Music & lyrics ©Laurian Taler, 2013

A1
Why do we ask always
In this unknown life maze
What is the meaning of love
What is the meaning of love
Is it a mixture of feelings
With the attraction to one
As I want you so much
Or is it just
The huge self-love that I hide
Within a play that might work
Left inside me
From games of survival
That some ancestors played
I recognize it is not very savvy
To ask about love
A2
Instead of asking of
Words that are so deep, like
What is the meaning of love
What is the meaning of love
We should hold hands and together
Soak up of each other's gaze
Until souls are ablaze
Then dance embraced
As the birds of the sky
Before they build their nest
And change the moments
That make us happy
In timeless desire
To break the code of the powerful meaning
The answer to love

2709. CAN'T BE HAPPY
IF PEOPLE ARE HUNGRY

Music & lyrics ©Laurian Taler, 2012

A1
Can't be happy if people are hungry
And if they are sick and starve to death
Can't be happy if people are homeless
Let us rise against unfairness

A2
Can't be happy if we don't do something
To eradicate hunger around
If we do not build a better planet
Goods for everybody to abound

B1
Come, work together to share the wealth,
Ask for the rules now to change,
Freedom, a home, and enough bread and health
And make more decent the gap in a small range

A1

A3
Can't be happy if we don't do something
To eradicate hunger around
Let us all now build a better planet
Share the wealth,
Share the wealth,
Share the wealth,
Share the wealth, or else!

2710. PASSION RUNS ME

Music & lyrics ©Laurian Taler, 2013

A
Passion runs me with a fervour
Changing fever into chills
Passion runs me with a fervour
Changing anger into thrills
'Cause I want to stroke your soul
To quench down my love thirst
To round you with my feelings

Passion runs me with a fervour
You embody what I seek

B (2x)
Between me and you
There are
Deep connections that
Go far
Between me and you
Are ties
That only I see
Into your eyes

2801. SPRING SEEMS LATE

Music & lyrics ©Laurian Taler, 2013

A1
Spring seems late this year
Why, it is not too clear
But my heart is hot
You warmed it on the spot
A2
Spring seems late this year
The snowdrops aren't near
But a flower grew
It is my love for you
B
Without spring or any season
I am mad for you
Be it March or late November
My mind is askew
Days and nights are lonely
If you are not near
Keep the spring in my life
Be with me, my dear
C1
When your eyes that shine with promise
Look into my eyes
Be it snow or hail or thunder
I'm getting my highs
C2
When you softly say the sweet words
I don't need no spring
'Cause your eyes and voice and laughter
Make me want to sing

A1, A2, B

2802. SNOW RUSH

Music & lyrics ©Laurian Taler, 2014

Slow waltz

A1
We looked, caught in wonder
How snow rushed the car
It turned into a mantle
That took us so far
To dreams full of beauty
To dreams full of love

Snow rushed on us from above, Oh
Snow rushed on us from above, Oh
Love was on us like a glove, Oh

B
It took an eon, a wink,
We didn't even dare to blink
The snow rush turned us to dream
One of the life moments supreme (3x)
Yeah!

A2
Don't drive out in winter
Confronting snowstorms
It is better to splinter
From your dreams in your dorms
'Cause dreams in the snow rush
Will melt as a fling

Love is eternal in spring, Oh (3x)

2803. ECHO OF YOUTH

Music & lyrics ©Laurian Taler, 2014

A1
The sounds of other time
And the songs full of sweet rhyme
In the fields where we walked
Holding hands while we talked
Kisses in the woods that gave us shade
All your laughs and your smiles for me

A2
The sky bluer than blue
The horizons without clue
And the passion that so grew
For a life, right and true
Kisses in the woods that gave us shade
All your laughs and your smiles for me

B (2x)
With the echo of my youth vibrating
With the echo of my youth alive
Glimpses of our strive
In my mind revive
What was for both fascinating
Time

2201. WE HAVE HAD SO MANY DAYS

Music & lyrics ©Laurian Taler, 2005

A
We have had so many days,
So many nights of bliss,
We have shared tenderness,
A hold of hands, a kiss,

Then we went each other way
Into the dream called life
Missing on what we'd have been
Loving husband and wife.

B
Where are the days
And sumptuous nights
Of bliss
Who can look at you
And worship you
As heaven on earth
I miss the silent embrace,
Kiss on your eyes
I miss the flutter that
In my chest
Spoke of love

A, B

2601. VIOLLAD

A1
I feel in my lone heart
A ballad with low strings
I feel in my lone heart
A sky bird with no wings

B1
It sings a slow tune
Trembling in night
It is not immune
To the lonely soul
With desperation fright

C
Ballad, don't cry for lonely hearts
Who sing loud to blue moons
Ballad, take trembling out of parts
And better sing me happy tunes

A, B,

C + Life's a blast !

UNDER THE BLUE SKY
LYRICS FROM MY SONGS

©Laurian Taler, 2014

GONG PUBLISHING
TORONTO

www.gongnog.com

ISBN 978-1-926477-03-9

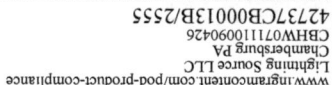